steaming

steaming

brigid treloar

PERIPLUS

Contents

Introduction to steaming

Traditionally, if you mentioned steaming, people would think only of steamed vegetables. But times have changed. The emphasis today is on light, healthy cooking methods that allow the flavor of food to stand out. Steaming suits this trend perfectly. The natural taste and shape of food is retained, and light flavorings, seasonings and sauces are used to enhance, not to dominate. The taste and aroma of herbs, spices and other condiments are gently steamed into the food.

Steaming comes from an ancient method of cooking that used the stones of hot springs. One of the earliest examples of a steaming utensil is a *hsein*, a two-part bronze steamer (now in the British Museum), thought to have first been used by the Chinese in the 11th and 12th centuries B.C. The cooking method of steaming quickly spread from China to South-East Asia, then to Japan and India, and on to Europe and Britain, each country adding its own flavors and special ingredients and adjusting the methods and cooking times to suit its own cuisine. The South-East Asian countries used bamboo steamers and woks; the Europeans used steaming baskets and fish kettles, reducing the juices mixed with the steaming liquid to a sauce; the British steamed their suet puddings wrapped in floured cloths, and the Scots their haggis in a sheep's stomach. Steaming was here to stay.

One of the gentlest methods of cooking, steaming suits a wide range of foods and yields subtle, moist and aromatic results. The even heat of the simmering liquid's vapors gently envelops the food resting above in a perforated container, and allows the food to retain most of its natural juices, flavor, color, vitamins and minerals, which would otherwise be lost in the cooking water. The use of fat is unnecessary, and steamed food is light and healthy.

As a general rule, the cooking time in a microwave is slightly less. Remember food will continue to cook after being removed from a microwave, so it is always better to slightly undercook, because standing time may be sufficient to complete the cooking. Check occasionally, until food is cooked to personal preference. It can always be cooked longer, if required.

Steaming is a surprisingly easy way to cook, without the need for expensive equipment. So, if you haven't yet tried steaming, follow some of the recipes in this book. You will be pleasantly surprised.

Equipment for steaming

Many types of equipment can be used for steaming, ranging from the expensive to the extremely cheap. Foods can also be cooked in their own steam without any added liquid. They can be placed in a casserole dish or a saucepan with a tight-fitting lid over low heat, or wrapped into a "parcel" and placed in a steamer. If food is wrapped, allow a little more cooking time.

Steamer baskets and pots

Stovetop steamers, with one or two handles, come in many sizes, shapes, materials and prices. The steamer basket can be bought separately, or in sets with a base saucepan, but usually there is only one lid for the set. Aluminum, stainless steel, or enamel steaming baskets, fit snugly into standard-sized saucepans to steam on the stovetop. (The different bases of saucepans transfer heat differently; the more efficient, the more expensive.) Some steamer baskets have a ridged base that fits a number of different-sized saucepans snugly, allowing no steam to escape. The ridging does mean that the diameter of the base is smaller than the diameter of the top, a disadvantage as some food may have to be overlapped to fit, and could cover all the steam holes. These types of steamer baskets are usually quite deep, which can make it difficult to remove the food after it is cooked. Layer food according to cooking times, that requiring the longest on the bottom.

A pasta pot with a deep, perforated basket with handles doubles well as a steamer. The "multifunctional" pot has an additional shallow perforated basket that fits snugly on top as a steaming basket. It's worthwhile to purchase such a versatile set.

Multi-tiered aluminum or stainless steel steamer sets, available in Asian stores, are multipurpose. With a base and usually two steaming baskets they can be used to cook a whole meal. The light-gauge aluminum is not very sturdy; spend the extra money and buy stainless steel.

Although traditionally used to poach whole fish, fish kettles can be used to steam quantities of foods with short cooking times, such as corn on the cob.

The perforated tray is so close to the bottom that you will have to refill it often with water.

Bamboo steamers

One of the cheapest and most attractive utensils for steaming is the two-level bamboo steamer, available in many sizes from Asian supermarkets and specialty cookware shops. The open-slat base allows steam to circulate easily and efficiently. The lid has an almost perfect design, allowing excess steam to escape through the tightly woven bamboo, with little condensed steam dripping back onto the food. The depth of the bamboo steamer, especially the smaller ones, could be a limitation for some cooking. Alternatively, cover the steamer with foil instead of the lid, or turn another bamboo basket upside down over the food—this will allow extra height—and then cover with the lid.

A 12-inch (30-cm) steamer fits perfectly into a standard 14-inch (35-cm) wok, and easily holds a dinner plate for steaming whole fish. Slower-cooking foods are placed in the bottom level and faster cooking in the one above; also, to even cooking times, you could change the baskets around during the cooking process. An entire meal can be prepared at once, or the same dish can be cooked in several batches.

A few points to remember when using a bamboo steamer:

- Soak new steamers in cold water for *at least* 2 hours before use, to clean thoroughly.
- If there are large gaps between the bamboo slats, place the food on a plate, parchment (baking) paper, or leaves.
- If you are lining the steamer, leave some space on the base to allow steam to circulate efficiently.
- Bamboo steamers look good enough to serve from at the table, but should be placed over a plate to catch drips.

To clean a bamboo steamer, simply rinse it in hot water after each use and dry thoroughly before storing in an airy place. If cooked food is to be left in the steamer for any length of time before serving, place a tea towel under the lid to catch any condensation. If the lid is a bit loose when cooking, wrap a damp towel around it to stop steam from escaping.

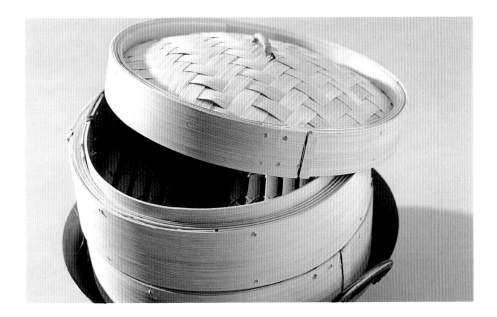

Collapsible steaming plates and steaming baskets

Cheap, easy to store, and available in different sizes, collapsible aluminum and stainless steel steaming baskets fold out to fit inside saucepans. Most have a removable handle and small feet. There is not much room for water underneath the baskets, so you should check the water level regularly.

To steam small portions in a saucepan, if you are cooking for only one or two, perforated dishes with feet and a handle are very useful. Available in specialty cookware shops.

Electric steamers

These two-tiered, plug-in steamers can cook larger quantities of food at once, or even a whole meal. Put meat and fish in the lower steamer and vegetables at the top. A timer reminds you to turn this steamer off, which is good, as it cooks faster than most others. Some even have an alarm that will go off if the water starts to boil dry.

For cooks who have everything, there are now built-in steamers just like those restaurants use. They are fast and efficient, but expensive.

Electric rice steamers

Some Asian countries use what looks like an upside-down bamboo hat that sits over a pot of simmering liquid to steam glutinous rice to perfection. For most people however, an electric rice cooker is the way to go. Besides cooking rice perfectly, it can be used as a steamer. The steaming rack is placed in the cooker with the appropriate amount of water. If no rack is supplied, use a cake rack, trivet or upside-down bowl. Place food on the steaming rack and cover with the lid, then switch on the cooker. Once the rice is cooked the device automatically switches to the warm cycle; however, the food should be served as close to cooking time as possible.

Do-it-yourself steamers

If no special steaming equipment is available, simply improvize with what you already have in the kitchen. A metal colander or sieve over a large pot of simmering water—make sure it does not touch the water—can work just as well as the most expensive equipment. Wrap a tea towel around the edge to fill any gaps between the colander and saucepan where steam might escape. If no lid is available, just cover the pan tightly with foil.

No metal colander? Place a cake rack, upside-down bowl or trivet in the pot so it is above the level of the water. Put the plate of food to be cooked on top, and cover the pot with a tight-fitting lid or foil.

Couscousières

The Moroccan couscousière is traditionally used as a casserole to cook vegetables, fish, or meat in the base while the couscous is steamed in the perforated top section. It can also be used as a regular steamer, with simmering liquid in the lower section.

Pressure cookers (infusion cookers)

The traditional pressure cookers are now often called infusion cookers, but the principle is exactly the same: pressurized steam in a sealed pan can halve the normal cooking time. Some much-needed safety features have been added. If too much steam builds up, a valve is automatically opened to release it, and the lid cannot be removed until the pressure has dropped. This is a great improvement on old-fashioned pressure cookers, which could cause accidents if the lid was removed before the pressure had dropped. Steamer baskets are an extra, but are very useful, especially for small quantities of food.

Steaming tips

Whether you are using the latest in steaming equipment, or a do-it-yourself steamer, there are a few basic tips to remember. One of the most important things to note is that only the highest quality ingredients should be used when steaming food, as steaming accentuates the slightest doubtful odor or blemish.

Steaming tips

1. If the food is likely to release juices, place it in a shallow bowl or deep plate; the juices can be used as a sauce.

2. Steam over medium heat, keeping the water at a rapid simmer. To be alerted to a low water level, place 2 or 3 marbles or coins in the base of the steamer. The gentle knocking sound they make in boiling water will stop when the water level drops too low.

3. Unless browned first, food that is steamed will be flavorful and succulent, but pale in color. Simply serve with a sauce or garnish to add color.

4. Cooking time can be shortened if the food is cut into small pieces. For even cooking, make sure the pieces are about the same size.

5. Cooking is timed from the moment the food is placed in the steamer over the already simmering water and covered. Make sure the lid is firmly in place so that no steam escapes.

6. When you steam meat, the steam will cause fat to melt and fall into the simmering liquid, thereby reducing the fat content.

7. Steamed whole fish retains its shape better than fish cooked in liquid. However, be careful when lifting it out. Placing a whole fish on parchment (baking) paper or a leaf makes removal easier. Scrunch up the paper around the fish, or leave it on the leaf to serve.

8. Parchment (baking) paper and leaves can also be cut to fit under small pieces of food, such as dumplings, allowing steam to circulate efficiently.

9. Do not sprinkle salt over vegetables, as it draws moisture out during cooking and may discolor them.

The steaming liquid

Water is the most common steaming medium, but stock, beer, wine and other liquids can be used to impart subtle flavors. To make an infusion, bring liquid to a rapid simmer and drop in a bunch of fresh herbs; then remove the pot from the heat. Leave to infuse for 20 minutes before reheating to use as the steaming liquid.

Flavored steaming liquids can be strained into a small saucepan after the food is cooked, then reduced and used or added to a sauce.

Step-by-step steaming method

1. Oil the base of a bamboo steamer or steamer basket, or simply line the steamer with parchment (baking) paper or leaves to prevent food from sticking. Do not cover the base completely, as some space must be left for steam to circulate efficiently. For dumplings and buns, you can cut individual pieces of parchment (baking) paper.

2. Place the food to be cooked in the bamboo steamer or steamer basket. Always keep the food about 1 inch (2.5 cm) from the sides of the steamer.

3. Partially fill a wok or pot with water and bring to a rapid simmer. The base of the steamer should be just above the level of the simmering liquid and should not touch the liquid.

4. Cover and steam until the food is cooked. Occasionally check the water level, adding more boiling water if necessary. Remove the steamer or basket from the wok or pot before removing the food.

Ingredients

The recipes in this book require a number of ingredients that are commonly found in the modern kitchen and easily available in local and Asian stores. In the cooking method, kitchen towels, parchment (baking) paper, ramekins (can be substituted with Chinese teacups), and small dishes are also called for, to place inside a bamboo steamer or steamer basket. It's a good idea to have these items handy before beginning a recipe.

Wrappers and liners

Wrapping food and placing it on a heat source is as ancient as cooking itself. While wrapped food takes a little longer to cook, wrapping adds an extra flavor that enhances simple meals, and creates a great presentation. Green leaves such as lettuce, cabbage, grape, and spinach create a flavorsome, edible wrap, while banana, palm, lotus leaves, and corn husks are inedible, though they impart their flavor and protect the food and its shape. Both of these types of wrappers can also be used as liners.

Because leaves hold in moisture, leaf parcels reheat well, often have a better flavor the day after being cooked, and are easy to handle. Use string to tie parcels.

Functional wrappers and liners that stop food from sticking, but impart no flavor to food are aluminum foil and parchment (baking) paper. When using foil, always oil it first and wrap with the shiny side facing in. Because wrappers are insulated, allow slightly longer cooking time for wrapped food, or raise the temperature a little so the cooking time remains the same.

Wrappers

Inedible: Banana leaves, pandanus leaves, bamboo leaves, lotus leaves, aluminum foil, parchment (baking) paper, oven bags

Edible: Rice paper wrappers, wonton wrappers (square or round), pot sticker (gow gee) wrappers, cabbage leaves, spinach leaves, grape leaves, bean curd sheets, seasoned tofu (bean curd) pouches, crepes, nori (seaweed)

Appetizers and starters

Steaming starters and appetizers makes good sense. Think ahead and make ahead, then simply refrigerate until serving—pâtés, terrines, dips, savory mousses, marinated steamed vegetables, or vegetable salads.

If you are serving hot food, many dishes can be prepared ahead and reheated in a covered steamer over boiling water when needed. You can also double-stack steamers and cook a starter with another course. Soups, stuffed peppers, tomatoes and eggplants, savory soufflés, crêpe and rice paper parcels, vegetables, and seafood make delectable steamed starters.

Dim sum, a steamed or deep-fried Chinese snack, is traditionally eaten between meals or for lunch. The sweet and savory dumplings, wontons, steamed buns and parcels wrapped in egg or bean curd sheets are often served in the bamboo steamers they were cooked in. Invest in a few small bamboo steamers and serve one for each person. If you are double-stacking steamers remember to rotate food on the two levels to cook evenly.

Wrappers are interchangeable in most recipes (see list page 14). Substitute wonton or pot sticker (gow gee) wrappers for blanched cabbage or spinach leaves, or use bean curd sheets or rice paper wrappers.

In this chapter, we have included some wonderful ideas for meal appetizers, that can also be used in parties as hors d'oeuvres. Recipes such as the mouth-watering chili-chicken dumplings and ginger-sesame pork rolls have a distinctly Asian flavor, and showcase the lightness, texture and flavorsome results you can achieve with steaming. You can interchange the chicken for pork, or the ginger for chili. The ingredients are easily found and the wrappers make these starters beautiful to serve.

The hazelnut and watercress pumpkin soup and the chicken balls on rosemary sprigs are two other delicious examples of how to present food in a creative, yet simple way.

The varieties and possibilities are endless. Try expanding on the ideas within this book and interchange ingredients. Your imagination is the only limit!

Chili-chicken dumplings

8 oz (250 g) ground (minced) chicken

4 scallions (shallots/spring onions), finely chopped

¼ clove garlic, crushed

¼ cup (1 ½ oz/45 g) roasted peanuts, finely chopped

¼ cup (⅓ oz/10 g) fresh cilantro (fresh coriander) leaves, chopped

1 tablespoon sweet chili sauce

2 teaspoons soy sauce

½ teaspoon fish sauce

16 round wonton or pot sticker (gow gee) wrappers

chili sauce

For chili sauce

¼ cup (2 fl oz/60 ml) rice vinegar

¼ cup (2 fl oz/60 ml) fresh lime juice

2 teaspoons fish sauce

1 tablespoon packed palm or brown sugar

1 tablespoon water

1 clove garlic, crushed

1 small fresh red chili, seeded and finely chopped (leave seeds in for more heat)

Variation: To make these into flower dumplings, fill wrapper, then gather edges around filling, forming a basket, and gently squeeze center of dumpling to expose the filling at the top. Tap bottom of dumpling on work surface to flatten. Repeat with remaining wrappers.

In a bowl, combine chicken, scallions, garlic, peanuts, cilantro, chili sauce, soy sauce and fish sauce. Place wrappers on a work surface and cover with a damp kitchen towel. Take each wrapper and place in a gow gee press or place 1 wrapper on a work surface. Spoon 2 teaspoons filling in center of wrapper. Brush edges of wrapper with water, and close seal of press, or fold in half, pressing with fingers to seal and make a frilled edge. Cover with a damp kitchen towel and repeat with remaining wrappers and filling.

Place dumplings in a steamer or steamer basket lined with parchment (baking) paper, leaving some space for steam to circulate efficiently. Partially fill a wok or pot with water (steamer or basket should not touch water) and bring to a rapid simmer. Place steamer over boiling water and cover. Steam for 10 minutes. Serve dumplings warm with chili sauce.

To make chili sauce: Combine ingredients, stirring constantly until sugar dissolves.

Makes 16

Ginger-sesame pork rolls

8 oz (250 g) ground (minced) pork

3 scallions (shallots/spring onions),
finely chopped

2 tablespoons chopped canned
bamboo shoots

1 teaspoon peeled and grated fresh ginger

¼ teaspoon five-spice powder

2 teaspoons soy sauce

1 teaspoon Asian sesame oil

8 bean curd sheets, 5 by 6 inches
(13 by 15 cm)

¼ small red bell pepper (capsicum),
seeded and thinly sliced

4 scallions (shallots/spring onions), green
tops only, cut into 5-inch (13-cm) lengths

For hoisin and ginger sauce

¼ cup (2 fl oz/60 ml) hoisin sauce

2 tablespoons shaoxing wine or
dry sherry

2 teaspoons chopped fresh ginger

1 clove garlic, crushed

1 scallion (shallot/spring onion),
finely chopped

Variation: Steam 8 savoy
cabbage leaves for 2 minutes
to soften. Drain and use in place
of tofu to wrap pork.

Place pork, scallions, bamboo shoots, ginger, five-spice powder, soy sauce, and sesame oil in a bowl and mix until well combined. Lightly brush bean curd sheets with cold water and lay flat on a work surface. Spread ⅛ of mixture along one end of each sheet. Lay strips of red bell pepper and scallions along meat and push gently until completely enclosed by meat. Fold two sides of sheet in and roll up, brushing remaining side lightly with water if needed. Press down firmly to seal.

Partially fill a large wok or pot with water (steamer should not touch water) and bring to a rapid simmer.

Line a bamboo steamer or steamer basket with parchment (baking) paper or leaves, leaving some space for steam to circulate efficiently. Arrange tofu rolls in a single layer in steamer. Place steamer over water, cover, and cook until pork mixture is firm and ready, about 10 minutes.

Remove rolls from steamer. Serve whole or cut into diagonal pieces and stand with cut side up, with hoisin and ginger sauce for dipping.

To make hoisin and ginger sauce: Combine all ingredients in a bowl, and mix well.

Makes 8 rolls

Hazelnut and watercress pumpkin soup

4 golden nugget butternut squash (pumpkin), 3½ lb (1.8 kg) total

1 tablespoon butter or vegetable oil

2 cloves garlic, crushed

1 small yellow (brown) onion, chopped

1 teaspoon peeled and grated fresh ginger

4 cups (32 fl oz/1 L) chicken or vegetable stock

salt and pepper to taste

4 teaspoons plain (natural) yogurt or sour cream

12 sprigs watercress

½ cup (2½ oz/75 g) hazelnuts, toasted, skinned and coarsely chopped

Variation: Omit hazelnuts and add 8 medium shrimp (prawns), peeled, deveined and chopped, to garlic and shallots. Cover and steam until cooked and soup is bright orange, 3–4 minutes.

Partially fill a large wok or pot with water (steamer or basket should not touch water) and bring to a rapid simmer. Place whole squash in oiled steamer. Place steamer over water, cover, and steam until squash are just tender, 40–45 minutes. Remove steamer from wok before removing squash.

Place squash on a board, flatter side down (take care, as it will be hot). Cut tops off and discard. Discard seeds, and scoop out flesh to within ¼ inch (6 mm) of skin, being careful not to break through. Turn squash upside down to drain, adding any drained juice to flesh. Purée squash flesh. Cover shells with foil to keep warm.

Heat butter or oil in a medium saucepan over medium heat. Cook garlic, onion and ginger until softened but not brown, 4–5 minutes. Add puréed squash, stock, and salt and pepper, and simmer for 10 minutes. Pour soup into shells and serve garnished with yogurt, watercress, and hazelnuts.

Tip: Squash and soup can be prepared the day before serving and chilled. If reheating soup in a saucepan, steam squash for 10–15 minutes to heat through before filling with hot soup. To reheat soup in shells by steaming, allow 45 minutes.

Serves 4

Chicken balls on rosemary sprigs

8 woody sprigs rosemary, about 5–6 inches long (13–15 cm)

12 oz (375 g) ground (minced) chicken

1 small onion, finely diced

2 cloves garlic, crushed

2 tablespoons plain (natural) yogurt

1 teaspoon ground cumin

1 tablespoon chopped fresh cilantro (fresh coriander)

1 tablespoon chopped fresh mint

2 teaspoons cornstarch (cornflour)

pinch salt and freshly ground black pepper

For yogurt and mint sauce

1 cup (8 oz/250 g) plain (natural) yogurt

1 tablespoon finely chopped fresh mint

1 small green cucumber, finely chopped

1 tablespoon fresh lemon juice

2 cloves garlic, crushed

pinch salt and freshly ground black pepper

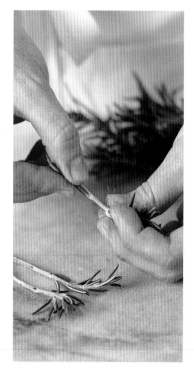

Cut each rosemary sprig in half, stripping off all the leaves except for a tuft at one end. Wash and pat dry with paper towels. Place chicken, onion, garlic, yogurt, cumin, cilantro, mint, cornstarch, salt, and pepper in a bowl and mix until well combined. With damp hands, shape about 1 tablespoon of mixture firmly around each rosemary sprig. Place in steamer or steamer basket on individual pieces of parchment (baking) paper.

Partially fill a wok or pot with water (steamer should not touch water) and bring to a rapid simmer.

Place steamer over water, cover, and steam until balls are cooked, about 10 minutes.

To make yogurt and mint sauce: Combine all ingredients in a bowl and mix well.

Serve sprigs on a banana leaf, with yogurt and mint dipping sauce.

Makes 16 balls

Rice, noodles and grains

Most grains and pulses steam well, although some require soaking before cooking, which softens the grains and reduces the cooking time. Always leave rice in a covered steamer for 5–10 minutes after cooking, to allow all moisture to be completely absorbed, and soggy patches to disappear. If a softer rice is preferred, leave cooked rice to sit a little longer.

To reheat rice: Place rice in a heatproof bowl and sit in a bamboo steamer or steamer basket. Place over rapidly simmering water, cover, and steam until heated through, 10–15 minutes. Rice will become quite firm and chewy if refrigerated.

In this book we have used sticky rice (another name for glutinous rice), sushi rice (made with short- or medium-grain rice) and black glutinous rice. Glutinous rice becomes sticky and sweet when cooked; black glutinous rice becomes a light purple color when cooked.

Lentils: Lentils cook very well in a steamer after soaking. Some need to be soaked longer than others. The masoor dhal, or red lentil, is the quickest to cook and can be eaten as a dip with raw vegetables or pita bread, or simply as an accompaniment to an Indian meal.

Couscous: These days most Westerners opt for the convenience of using instant couscous. Those without their own couscousière can simply use a bamboo steamer or steamer basket lined with cheesecloth (muslin) that fits snugly into a large wok or pot.

A general guide for steaming times:

Rice: Steamed white rice 20–25 minutes; steamed brown rice 35–45 minutes; black and white glutinous rice 40–45 minutes

Chickpeas: Soaked, for 60 minutes

Lentils: Unsoaked, for 40–45 minutes; soaked (30–60 minutes), for 25–30 minutes

Couscous: Soaked (10 minutes), for 30 minutes

Instant couscous: Soaked (4–5 minutes), for 10–15 minutes

Noodles (cooked, not steamed): Fresh udon and egg noodles 2–3 minutes; dried egg noodles 5 minutes; dried udon noodles 6–10 minutes (different sizes available); dried Italian pasta 8–10 minutes

Perfect steamed rice

Method 1:

in steamer

1 cup (7 oz/220 g) long-grain white rice

1¼ cups (10 fl oz/310 ml) cold
water or stock

Put rice in a fine-meshed sieve and
rinse under cold running water. Let
drain for 5 minutes, then place in a
heatproof bowl that fits in steamer.
Add water. Fill a wok or pot with water
(water should not touch steamer) and
bring to a rapid simmer. Place steamer
over water, cover, and steam rice until
tender and water has evaporated,
20–25 minutes. Remove pot or wok
from heat. Place a cloth under lid to
stop any condensation dripping back
onto rice, and let stand for 5–10
minutes. Fluff rice with a fork and
serve. If not using rice immediately,
refrigerate, and reheat when needed.

Serves 2–3

Variation: Cook rice with a
small pinch of saffron threads,
a pinch of ground saffron, or
ground turmeric, or add a little
grated ginger.

Method 2:

in liquid in pot, with meat
or vegetables steaming above

2 cups (16 fl oz/500 ml) cold water or stock

1 cup (7 oz/220 g) long-grain white rice

Bring water to boil in a pot. Add rice, stirring well,
and reduce heat to a rapid simmer. Place a
bamboo steamer or steamer basket with meat or
vegetables inside over water, cover, and steam
until liquid is absorbed, 12–15 minutes. Remove
from heat and stand, covered, for 5–10 minutes.
Fluff with a fork and serve. If not using immediately,
refrigerate rice, and reheat when needed.

Serves 2–3

Note: If cooking more than 1 cup long grain rice
only add 1½ cups liquid per cup rice after the first
cup.

Herbed rice: Cook 1 cup (7 oz/220 g) long-grain
rice according to one of the above recipes. Gently
fold in ⅓ cup (½ oz/15 g) finely chopped fresh
herbs such as parsley or cilantro (coriander).

Sushi rice

1 ½ cups (10 oz/300 g) short- or
medium-grain rice

1 ½ cups (12 fl oz/375 ml) cold water

For sushi vinegar

¼ cup (2 fl oz/60 ml) rice vinegar

2 tablespoons sugar

¼ teaspoon salt

Wash rice in 3 or 4 changes of cold water until
water is clear. Let drain for 5 minutes, then place
in a bowl that fits in bamboo steamer or steamer
basket, and add water. Let soak for 30 minutes.
Place in steamer.

Partially fill a wok or pot with water (water should
not touch steamer) and bring to a rapid simmer.
Place steamer over water, cover, and steam until
cooked and water evaporated, 20–25 minutes.
Remove from heat and let stand for 10 minutes
with a cloth under the lid to stop any condensation
dripping back onto rice. If softer rice is preferred,
let rice stand slightly longer.

Put hot rice in a flat, shallow, non-metallic dish and
pour sushi vinegar over. With a wooden paddle or
spoon, slice through rice at a 45-degree angle to
break up any lumps and distribute vinegar evenly.
Fan cool for 5–8 minutes, turning rice 2 to 3 times
for even cooling. Cover with a damp kitchen towel
to stop rice drying out until served.

To make sushi vinegar: Combine ingredients in
a small bowl, stirring until sugar and salt dissolve
completely. Mixture can be heated over low heat if
required. (Sushi vinegar ingredients can be altered
according to taste.) Stir into hot cooked rice.

Makes about 4 ½ cups (22 ½ oz/675 g)

Sushi tofu pouches

2 tablespoons white sesame seeds, toasted

$\frac{1}{2}$ small English (hothouse) cucumber, seeded and chopped

Sushi rice (see page 30 for recipe)

20 seasoned tofu pouches (inari-zushi), from an Asian food store

$1\frac{1}{2}$ cups (12 fl oz/375 ml) cold water, for handling rice

$1\frac{1}{2}$ tablespoons rice vinegar, for handling rice

2 teaspoons wasabi paste, optional

20 sweet seasoned kampyo strips or 20 scallions (shallots/spring onions), green part only, blanched

2 tablespoons Japanese pickled ginger, from an Asian food store, optional

Note: Tofu pouches are ready to eat from the packet.

To toast sesame seeds: Toast seeds in a frying pan over medium heat until golden brown. Keep moving pan so seeds do not burn.

Add sesame seeds and cucumber to sushi rice, slicing through, not stirring, with a wooden paddle or spoon to mix evenly without squashing rice. Keep covered with a damp kitchen towel while preparing tofu pouches.

Tofu pouches are already cut on one side. Gently open cut side, easing your fingers inside to corners, and taking care not to break skin. Sushi rice is very sticky. Pour cold water into a small bowl and add rice vinegar. Dip fingers in before handling the rice. Shake off excess vinegar water. Pick up a small handful of rice, about $1\frac{1}{2}$ tablespoons, and place in pouch. Add a small dab of wasabi to rice (optional). Fold one side of pouch over rice, and then the other. Turn upside down so opening is on the bottom.

Lay a kampyo strip across a work surface, put pouch on top, and tie up loosely but carefully, as pouches can break easily. (If using scallions, first drop into boiling water to soften. Rinse under cold water and drain.) Serve pouches at room temperature, with pickled ginger if desired.

Makes 20 pouches

Creamy coconut black rice

1 cup (7 oz/220 g) black glutinous rice

1 cup (8 fl oz/250 ml) cold water

1 1/2 cups (12 fl oz/375 ml) thin coconut cream or coconut milk

1/3 cup palm or brown sugar

2 teaspoons grated lime or lemon zest

pinch salt

1 cup (8 fl oz/250 ml) thick coconut cream, optional

1 medium (12 oz/375 g) mango, peeled and sliced

Place rice in a bowl and add cold water to cover. Let soak overnight, drain, and rinse well under cold running water. Place rice and water in a bowl that fits in a bamboo steamer or steamer basket.

Partially fill a wok or pot with water (steamer should not touch water) and bring to a rapid simmer. Place steamer over water, cover, and steam until rice is tender, 40–45 minutes, stirring occasionally. Remove from heat and stir in thin coconut cream, sugar, lime zest, and salt. Cover and steam until thickened to consistency of hot cereal, 15–20 minutes. Swirl thick coconut cream through, if desired, and serve with sliced mango. Alternatively, cut a small cantaloupe (rockmelon) in half, scoop out seeds, and fill with rice.

Serves 4–6

Sticky rice in banana leaves

1 cup (7 oz/220 g) white glutinous rice

3 tablespoons palm or brown sugar

¾ cup (6 fl oz/180 ml) thin coconut
cream or coconut milk

12 banana leaf squares, about
6 inches (15 cm)

1 mango, peeled and sliced, or 1–2
Ladyfinger (sugar) bananas

juice of 1 lime

1 teaspoon grated lime zest

Cover rice with cold water and let soak overnight. Drain. Line a bamboo steamer or steamer basket with cheesecloth (muslin) and spread rice evenly on top.

Partially fill a wok or pot with water (steamer should not touch water) and bring to a rapid simmer.

Place steamer over water, cover, and steam until rice is tender, 40–45 minutes, adding more water to wok if required. Remove from heat.

Put rice in a bowl and stir in sugar and coconut cream. Drop banana leaves into boiling water for 30 seconds to soften. Rinse under cold water. Place 1 tablespoon rice in center of each square. Lay a slice of fresh mango or banana on rice with a drop or two of lime juice and a pinch of zest. Fold end of banana leaf over rice, then fold both sides in and roll so rice is fully enclosed. Close securely with string or toothpick. Repeat with remaining rice.

Place parcels in a bamboo steamer or steamer basket over water, cover, and steam for 15 minutes. Serve parcels whole or halved. Leaves are not eaten.

Makes 12 parcels

Savory rice bites

1 1/2 tablespoons tamarind pulp

1/2 cup (4 fl oz/125 ml) boiling water

1 cup (7 oz/220 g) white glutinous rice

2 teaspoons grated fresh turmeric

1 teaspoon finely peeled and grated
fresh ginger

3/4 cup (6 fl oz/180 ml) thin coconut
cream or coconut milk

2 scallions (shallots/spring onions),
finely chopped

1/4 cup (1/3 oz/10 g) fresh cilantro
(fresh coriander) leaves, finely chopped

3 kaffir lime leaves, spines removed,
finely chopped

1/4 teaspoon grated kaffir lime zest

1 red chili, seeded and finely
chopped, optional

6 oz (185 g) barbecued pork
(available from Asian food stores) or
barbecued chicken, sliced

Sweet chili, satay, or hoisin sauce,
for serving

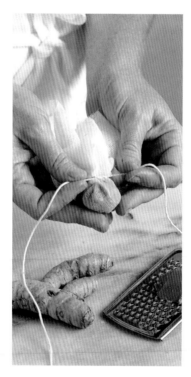

Place tamarind pulp in a small bowl and cover with boiling water. Mix well, breaking up pulp with a spoon to release flavor. Let stand for 5 minutes, then push through a fine-meshed strainer, discarding pulp and reserving liquid.

Wrap turmeric in a cheesecloth (muslin) square and tie with string. Put rice, turmeric and tamarind liquid in a medium bowl. Cover with cold water and let soak overnight. Drain, removing turmeric. Line a bamboo steamer or steamer basket with cheese-cloth (muslin) and spread rice evenly on top.

Partially fill a wok or pot with water (steamer should not touch water) and bring to a rapid simmer.

Place steamer over water, cover, and steam until rice is just tender, 30–35 minutes, adding more water to wok if required. Remove steamer from heat and put rice in a bowl.

Gently fold in ginger, coconut cream, scallions, cilantro, lime leaves, lime zest and chili. Spread rice evenly in an 8-inch (20-cm) square baking pan lined with parchment (baking) paper and refrigerate until set, about 2 hours. Cut into 16–20 squares to serve. Top with a small piece of barbecued pork or chicken and a dash of sweet chili, satay or hoisin sauce.

Makes 16–20 squares

Garlic and cumin lentils

1 cup (7 oz/220 g) masoor dhal
(dried red lentils)

2/3 cup (5 fl oz/150 ml) chicken stock
or water

1/2 teaspoon peeled and finely chopped
fresh ginger

1/2 teaspoon ground coriander

1 tablespoon ghee or vegetable oil

2 teaspoons toasted cumin seeds

1 medium onion (5 oz/150 g), sliced

2 cloves garlic, crushed

1 fresh long green chili, seeded and
thinly sliced, optional

1 tablespoon finely chopped fresh mint

Place lentils in a sieve and wash under cold running water. Pick over, and remove any foreign matter. Soak in water for a minimum of 1 hour. Drain well and place in a dish that will fit a bamboo steamer or steamer basket. Add stock, ginger and coriander, stir well, and place bowl in steamer.

Partially fill a wok or pot with water (steamer should not touch water) and bring to a rapid simmer. Place steamer over water, cover, and steam until lentils are soft, about 30 minutes.

Heat ghee in a medium pan and cook cumin seeds, onion, garlic and chili until onion browns, 8–10 minutes, stirring occasionally. Stir mint and half of onion mixture into lentils. Spread remaining onion mixture on top for garnish. Serve as a dip or side dish with crispy fried pappadums.

Makes about 2 1/4 cups (16 oz/500 g)

Tip: Lentils can be cooked for less time to retain shape (if not being mashed), and used in salads or as a vegetable.

Spicy vegetables on pistachio couscous

1 medium (18 oz/550 g) eggplant, cut into ½-inch (12-mm) pieces

coarse salt for sprinkling

2–3 tablespoons olive oil

1 large onion, chopped

2 cloves garlic, crushed

½ teaspoon each sweet paprika, ground cardamom, cumin, turmeric and cinnamon

2 medium tomatoes, chopped

10 oz (300 g) canned chickpeas, drained

6 cups (1½ lb/750 g) thickly sliced zucchini (courgette), carrots, cauliflower florets and green beans

2 tablespoons chopped mixed fresh herbs such as parsley, mint and cilantro (fresh coriander)

¾ cup (6 fl oz/180 ml) vegetable stock

For couscous

1 cup (6 oz/185 g) instant couscous

1½ cups (12 fl oz/375 ml) chicken stock

2 oz (60 g) butter, melted, or olive oil

½ cup (2 oz/60 g) pistachios, toasted and chopped

fresh parsley for garnish

Sprinkle eggplant with salt and let stand 30 minutes. Rinse under cold water, drain, and pat dry with paper towels. Heat oil in a large saucepan and sauté eggplant, onion and garlic until onion is softened but not brown, about 5 minutes. Add remaining ingredients to pan, cover, and simmer until vegetables are tender and flavors are well blended, 20–25 minutes, adding steaming basket with couscous for the last 10–15 minutes.

To make couscous: Heat stock in a small saucepan, remove from heat, and stir in couscous. Let stand until all liquid is absorbed, 4–5 minutes. Stir in butter or olive oil so couscous is evenly coated. Break up any lumps, and spread couscous out in a bamboo steamer or steamer basket lined with parchment (baking) paper. Place over vegetables, cover, and steam for 10–15 minutes to heat through. Stir in pistachios.

Serve couscous topped with vegetables and garnished with parsley.

Serves 4–6

To toast pistachios: Remove shells and place pistachios under a broiler (grill) or in a dry frying pan over medium heat and cook, stirring, until they just change color, 3–4 minutes. Be careful not to burn them.

Chicken with apricot and almond couscous stuffing

2 cups (12 oz/375 g) instant couscous

1½ cups 12 fl oz/375 ml) boiling water or stock

¾ cup (6 oz/180 g) butter or vegetable oil

2 cloves garlic, crushed

2 scallions (shallots/spring onions), finely chopped

2 teaspoons cumin seeds

pinch ground saffron

¼ cup (⅓ oz/10 g) chopped fresh cilantro (fresh coriander)

1¼ cups (8 oz/250 g) mixed dried raisins, dates and apricots

½ cup (2½ oz/75 g) pine nuts, toasted

¼ cup (⅓ oz/10 g) chopped fresh parsley

½ cup (2½ oz/75 g) slivered almonds, toasted (see page 94)

1 chicken, about 3 lb (1.5 kg)

For sherry sauce

1 cup (8 fl oz/250 ml) chicken stock

¼ cup (2 fl oz/60 ml) dry sherry or Madeira

1⅓ tablespoons cornstarch (cornflour)

2 teaspoons water

To toast pine nuts: Place nuts under a broiler (grill) or in a dry frypan over medium heat and cook, stirring, until they just change color, 3–4 minutes. Be careful not to burn them.

Put couscous in a medium bowl and pour boiling water over it. Let stand until all water is absorbed, 4–5 minutes. Heat butter in a small pan. Add garlic, scallions, cumin and saffron, and cook until fragrant, about 1 minute. Pour over couscous, mixing well. Stir in remaining ingredients and lightly pack into chicken. Close flap and secure with a skewer or toothpick. Put chicken in a bamboo steamer or steamer basket lined with lemon or lime leaves. If chicken is too high, turn another steamer upside down over it and then cover with a lid or greased foil.

Partially fill a wok or pot with water (steamer should not touch water) and bring to a rapid simmer. Place steamer over water and steam until cooked, 1¼–1½ hours, or until juices run clear when skewer is inserted in thigh. Chicken can be browned under broiler (grill) if desired, before serving with sherry sauce.

Place remaining couscous into oiled ramekins and steam with chicken. Let stand for 2 minutes before unmolding. Serve as an accompaniment to chicken.

Serves 4–6

To make sherry sauce: Heat stock and sherry in a small saucepan. Mix cornstarch and water, then add 1 tablespoon hot stock. Stir into remaining stock and cook, stirring, until thick.

Meat and poultry

Beef, veal, pork, lamb, and chicken cook quickly when steamed, so tougher cuts of meat are not suitable. Leave meat in covered steamer after cooking to allow juices to settle, making the meat tender and juicy (5–10 minutes).

Steamed meat and poultry will generally be colorless. If preferred, whole chickens and legs of lamb can be browned under the broiler (grill) before serving.

Roasts or whole chickens are large and will swell a little during cooking, so you can place another bamboo steamer or steamer basket upside down over the top, then cover with a lid.

To steam a complete meal, cook rice, pasta or potatoes in the liquid while meat is steaming above it.

Always remember to check after the minimum suggested time, whether meat is cooked, as it can be cooked longer if necessary.

A general guide for cooking times:

Poultry: Poussin (available at specialty butchers and poultry shops) 12–14 oz (375–450 g): 30–35 minutes Whole chicken 3 lb (1.5 kg): 50–55 minutes; boneless chicken breasts: 12–15 minutes; chicken legs: 15–20 minutes; chicken drumsticks: 12–15 minutes (allow 10–15 minutes extra cooking time for whole chickens with stuffing, 5 minutes extra for stuffed chicken pieces)

Meat: Cooking times will vary depending on preference for rare, medium or well-done meat. If meat is cooked over sliced vegetables such as potatoes, cooking time will be longer.

Beef roasts 10–12 minutes per lb (500 g), plus an extra 10–15 minutes; thinly sliced steak (sirloin): 3 minutes for medium rare (allow extra cooking time if steaks are rolled with filling); leg of lamb: 15 minutes per lb (500 g), plus an extra 10–15 minutes; chops:10–15 minutes; porkchops (average-sized): 15–18 minutes

Mini chili tomato meatballs with udon noodles

1 lb (500 g) ground (minced) beef

1 large onion, finely chopped

1 clove garlic, crushed

2½ tablespoons tomato paste

2 tablespoons Worcestershire sauce

2 tablespoons chopped fresh parsley

1 small red chili, seeded and finely chopped

1 egg, lightly beaten

salt and freshly ground pepper

25 oz (780 g) fresh udon noodles

¼ teaspoon salt

2 tablespoons olive oil

For sauce

light tomato sauce (see page 52)

1 small red chili, seeded and finely chopped, optional

2 tablespoons chopped fresh parsley

Variation: Toss meatballs in Basil Pesto (see page 56) instead of light tomato sauce.

Combine beef, onion, garlic, tomato paste, Worcestershire sauce, parsley, chili, egg, salt and pepper in a medium bowl, mixing well. Line a large bamboo steamer or steamer basket with parchment (baking) paper. With wet hands, take about 1 tablespoon mixture at a time and shape into small balls, and place in a single layer in steamer.

Partially fill a pot or wok with water (steamer should not touch water) and bring to a rapid simmer. Place steamer over water, cover, and steam until meatballs are cooked, 8–10 minutes. Add noodles and salt to water for the last 6 minutes of cooking, or until just tender. Drain noodles and toss with olive oil to keep from sticking.

While meatballs are cooking, heat tomato sauce in a small saucepan, adding chili if desired. Divide noodles among 4 plates and serve topped with meatballs and sauce, and sprinkled with parsley.

Serves 4

Marsala and mango chicken

4 boneless, skinless chicken thighs

1/2 cup (4 fl oz/125 ml) sweet Marsala

1 teaspoon five-spice powder

1 clove garlic, crushed

1 tablespoon peeled and grated
fresh ginger

1 mango, peeled and sliced

2 scallions (shallots/spring onions), cut
into 1 1/2-inch (4-cm) lengths

1/4 cup (1 oz/30 g) toasted pecans,
coarsely chopped

8 toothpicks

8 large spinach leaves

1 1/4 lb (20 oz/625 g) baby new potatoes

For marsala sauce

2 tablespoons butter or vegetable oil

1 clove garlic, crushed

2 tablespoons all-purpose (plain) flour

1 cup (8 fl oz/250 ml) chicken stock

reserved Marsala marinade

To make sauce: Melt butter in a small saucepan over medium heat and cook garlic for 1–2 minutes without browning. Add flour and cook, stirring constantly, until golden brown. Remove from heat and stir in chicken stock and reserved marsala marinade. Return to heat and simmer until mixture thickens.

Remove any excess fat from chicken. Put each chicken thigh between a double layer of plastic wrap and pound with a meat mallet until same thickness all over. Mix Marsala, five-spice, garlic and ginger. Pour over chicken, and refrigerate for at least 2 hours, or overnight. Turn chicken at least once.

Drain chicken, reserving marinade, and lay flat on a work surface. Put 2 or 3 slices of mango, 1/4 scallions and 1 tablespoon pecans on one end of each piece of chicken. Fold chicken over to enclose, and skewer closed at a 45-degree angle with 2 toothpicks. Hold each spinach leaf with tongs and plunge into boiling water until just softened, 2–3 seconds. Drain. Lay 4 leaves out flat on a work surface. Place chicken piece on each one, remove toothpicks, and cover with another leaf, shaping around chicken to enclose. Replace toothpicks. Place on individual pieces of parchment (baking) paper in steamer.

Partially fill a wok or pot with water (steamer should not touch water) and bring to a rapid simmer. Add potatoes to water. Place steamer on top, cover, and steam until potatoes and chicken are cooked (juices run clear when skewer is inserted in chicken thigh), 15–20 minutes. Meanwhile, make sauce. Slice rolls in half. Serve with potatoes, remaining sliced mango, and sauce.

Serves 4

Blue Castello and avocado chicken

4 boneless, skinless chicken breast halves

8 thin slices blue Castello or Gorgonzola cheese, about ¼ inch (6 mm) each

1 small avocado, peeled, pitted and sliced

2 scallions (shallots/spring onions), chopped

¼ cup (1 oz/30 g) chopped walnuts

1 bunch fresh lemon thyme or thyme

For light tomato sauce

3 large tomatoes, peeled and coarsely chopped

1 tablespoon olive oil

2 scallions (shallots/spring onions), chopped

1 clove garlic, crushed

2 teaspoons soy sauce

1 tablespoon lemon juice

2 teaspoons Worcestershire sauce

1 tablespoon chopped fresh basil or thyme

salt and cracked black pepper to taste

Variations: Cook chicken on thickly sliced fennel or spinach and serve as side dish. Or gently boil 1 ¼ lb (20 oz/600 g) baby new potatoes in liquid while chicken is steaming above.

Cut a slit along one side of each chicken breast to make a pocket. Lay 2 slices cheese, 2 slices avocado, ¼ scallions and nuts in each pocket. Skewer closed with a toothpick. Lay half the thyme in a bamboo steamer or steamer basket, with chicken on top. Spread remaining thyme over chicken.

Partially fill a wok or pot with water (steamer should not touch water) and bring to a rapid simmer. Place steamer over water, cover, and steam until cooked, 15–20 minutes (juices run clear when a skewer is inserted in thigh).

To skin tomatoes: Make a cut just through the skin around the center of each tomato. Plunge tomatoes into boiling water for 1 minute and immediately transfer to cold water. Peel skin off.

To make tomato sauce: Heat oil in a medium saucepan over medium-low heat. Add scallions and garlic and cook until soft but not brown, about 5 minutes. Reduce heat, stir in remaining ingredients, cover, and cook until thick, about 10 minutes. If a thinner sauce is preferred, add a little chicken stock.

Spoon tomato sauce over chicken, sprinkle with sprigs of lemon thyme, and serve with steamed rice or baby new potatoes.

Serves 4

Pork with mustard pear on potatoes and yams

3 tablespoons soy sauce

3 tablespoons honey

3 tablespoons sherry

4 pork chops, trimmed

4 teaspoons whole-grain (seed) mustard

1 firm pear, peeled, cored, and sliced into
¼-inch (6-mm) pieces

3–4 large potatoes (14 oz/440 g), cut
into ¼-inch (6-mm) pieces

2 medium yams or kumara (red sweet
potatoes), 12 oz (375 g) total, cut into
¼-inch (6-mm) pieces

2 large red (Spanish) onions, sliced into
¼-inch (6-mm) pieces

2 tablespoons olive oil

2 tablespoons chopped fresh herbs such
as sage, parsley, thyme or rosemary

salt and freshly ground black pepper
to taste

2 tablespoons chopped fresh parsley,
for garnish, optional

Mix soy, honey and sherry, and pour over pork chops. Cover and marinate for 1–2 hours, turning once. Drain, reserving marinade.

Spread 1 teaspoon mustard evenly over top of each pork chop. Arrange pear slices diagonally across each chop. In a bowl, toss potatoes, yams, onions, oil, herbs, salt and pepper, and spread evenly in a 12-inch (30-cm) bamboo steamer or steamer basket, with pork chops on top. It does not matter if potato slices overlap, but leave a small gap between potatoes and edge of steamer to allow steam to circulate efficiently.

Partially fill a wok or pot with water (steamer should not touch water) and bring to a rapid simmer. Place steamer over water, cover, and steam until chops and potatoes are cooked, 20–25 minutes depending on thickness. If chops cook through before potatoes, simply remove and keep warm until required. Boil marinade in a small saucepan. Serve pork with hot marinade, yams, and potatoes sprinkled with fresh parsley.

Serves 4

Tip: Steam green beans in a second steamer for last 10–12 minutes of cooking time and serve as a side dish.

Pesto and sun-dried tomato veal

For basil pesto

1 cup (1 oz/30 g) tightly packed fresh basil leaves

⅓ cup (2 oz/60 g) toasted pine nuts, (see page 44)

½ cup (2 oz/60 g) grated Parmesan

2 cloves garlic, crushed

salt and pepper to taste

½ cup (4 fl oz/125 ml) olive oil

skewers and toothpicks

4 veal scallops, about 5 oz (150 g) each, cut in half crosswise

½ cup (4 oz/125 g) oil-packed sun-dried tomatoes, drained

12–16 large spinach leaves

8 oz (250 g) mushrooms, stemmed and sliced

To make pesto: Place basil, pine nuts, Parmesan, garlic, salt, pepper and half of olive oil in a food processor, and purée. With machine running, gradually pour in remaining oil in a thin stream.

Pound veal with a meat mallet until thin, and lay flat on a work surface. Spread pesto over two-thirds of each piece, and place 3 or 4 sun-dried tomatoes at one end. Roll veal up and secure with a toothpick or skewer at a 45-degree angle. Hold each spinach leaf with tongs and plunge into boiling water just to soften, 2–3 seconds. Drain. Remove toothpick and wrap 1 leaf around each veal roll, overlapping 2 leaves if necessary. Secure toothpick again. Put mushrooms in a bamboo steamer or steamer basket lined with parchment (baking) paper, with veal on top.

Partially fill a wok or pot with water (steamer should not touch water) and bring to a rapid simmer. Place steamer over water, cover, and steam until just cooked through, 10–15 minutes. Remove toothpick.

Serve veal whole or cut diagonally, with cut side up to reveal colorful center. Serve with mushrooms and garlic mashed potatoes (see page 80 for recipe) or steamed rice.

Serves 4

Chicken, spinach and ginger dumplings

1 bunch spinach, stemmed, washed and chopped

8 oz (250 g) ground (minced) chicken

3 scallions (shallots/spring onions), finely chopped

1 teaspoon peeled and grated fresh ginger

2 cloves garlic, crushed

2 teaspoons soy sauce

1 teaspoon Asian sesame oil

1/2 teaspoon fish sauce

1 small red chili, seeded and finely chopped (optional)

3 teaspoons cornstarch (cornflour)

30 wonton wrappers

For chili sauce

1/4 cup (2 fl oz/60 ml) rice vinegar

2 tablespoons sugar

2 tablespoons water

1 teaspoon lemon juice

3/4 teaspoon fish sauce

1 small red chili, finely chopped (seeds removed for milder taste)

To make chili sauce: Combine ingredients, stirring constantly until sugar dissolves.

Put spinach in a bamboo steamer or steamer basket. Partially fill a wok or pot with water (steamer should not touch water), and bring to a rapid simmer. Put steamer over water, cover, and steam until spinach is soft, 2–3 minutes. Remove from heat and let cool. Squeeze out excess water and chop finely.

Put spinach in a medium bowl and add chicken, scallions, ginger, garlic, soy sauce, sesame oil, fish sauce, chili and cornstarch, mixing well.

Place wonton wrappers on work surface and cover with a damp kitchen towel. Working with 1 wrapper at a time, place 2 teaspoons filling in center and brush edges of wrapper with water. Gather edges together and twist to seal or fold wrapper in half, pressing edges together with fingers to seal. Cover with a damp kitchen towel and set aside. Repeat with remaining wrappers.

Line a large bamboo steamer or steamer basket with parchment (baking) paper. Partially fill a large wok or pot with water (steamer should not touch water) and bring to a rapid simmer. Arrange dumplings in steamer, making sure they do not touch. Place over water, cover, and steam for 10 minutes, adding more simmering water as necessary. Lift steamer off wok and carefully remove dumplings. Serve warm, with chili sauce.

Makes 30

Seafood

There is nothing quite as succulent and flavorsome as steamed seafood. However, it cooks surprisingly quickly, and so is very easy to overcook. Check at the minimum cooking time, because you can always cook it for a little longer if necessary. For added flavor, marinate before steaming, then reduce marinade and serve as a sauce.

Do not be limited by the seafood suggested in each recipe. In many cases, seafood types are interchangeable, only the cooking times may vary slightly. Cooking a large whole fish may be a problem without a fish kettle, so you may have to settle for two smaller fish that fit your bamboo steamer or steamer basket. Otherwise, try fish steaks, cutlets or fillets.

Steaming time is dictated more by the thickness of the fish than its weight. To test if it's cooked, insert a fork into the thickest part of the fish. If the flesh is opaque throughout and flakes easily, it's done. If the seafood is stuffed, wrapped, or cooked in a two-level steamer, allow extra cooking time and rotate the levels of the steamer halfway through for even cooking.

As a general guide, depending on size, cooking times are:

Whole fish: 10–15 minutes per lb (500 g)

Fish fillets: 5–8 minutes

Fish cutlets: 8–12 minutes

Mussels: 3–6 minutes

Prawns: 3–6 minutes

Scallops: 2–3 minutes

Australian Balmain bugs: 8–12 minutes

Lobster: 10–15 minutes

Snapper with hazelnuts and orange glaze

For marinade

1 tablespoon soy sauce

juice and grated zest of 1 orange

4 small whole snapper or trout, 8–12 oz (250–375 g) each

1 tablespoon butter or olive oil

1 large leek, washed and thinly sliced, green tops reserved

1 clove garlic, crushed

2 oranges, sliced

For glaze

⅓ cup (3 fl oz/90 ml) orange marmalade

1 tablespoon soy sauce

2 teaspoons water

For garnish

½ cup (2½ oz/75 g) hazelnuts, toasted and coarsely chopped

2 tablespoons chopped fresh parsley

To toast hazelnuts: Toast in a preheated 350°F (180°C/Gas 4) oven, for 8–10 minutes. Fold in a kitchen towel and rub together to remove skins.

Mix soy sauce, orange juice and zest in a small bowl. Pour over fish in a flat dish. Marinate for 30 minutes, turning once. Meanwhile, melt butter in a medium pan over medium heat and sauté leek and garlic until softened but not browned, 3–4 minutes. Let cool.

Make 3 diagonal slashes on each side of fish for even cooking. Fill fish cavities with sautéed leeks. Lay 1 or 2 overlapped green leek tops on a work surface for each fish. Top with half the orange slices, then the fish. Scatter the remaining orange slices on top. Place 2 fish in each level of a large 12-inch (30-cm) two-level steamer, and cover.

Partially fill a large wok or pot with water (steamer should not touch water) and bring to a rapid simmer. Place two-level steamer over water and steam until fish flakes when tested with a fork and flesh is opaque, 10–12 minutes, depending on thickness. Rotate levels of steamer halfway through for even cooking.

Meanwhile, make glaze: Heat marmalade, soy sauce and water in a small saucepan. Place fish on plates and discard orange slices. Pour hot glaze over top and garnish with hazelnuts and chopped parsley. Serve with crisp salad greens and herbed rice (see page 28 for recipe).

Serves 4

Thai curry fish in banana leaf cups

2–3 large banana leaves, cut into six 6-inch (15-cm) rounds

1 lb (500 g) white fish fillets, finely diced

2 tablespoons Thai red curry paste (available from Asian food stores)

1 tablespoon chopped roasted peanuts

1 cup (8 oz/250 ml) thick coconut cream

2 eggs, lightly beaten

1 tablespoon fish sauce

salt and pepper to taste

1 cup (3 oz/90 g) Chinese cabbage leaves, finely shredded

2 tablespoons thick coconut cream, for garnish, optional

1 fresh long red chili, seeded and thinly sliced for garnish, optional

Drop each banana leaf round into hot water to soften, 30–60 seconds. Drain and pat dry with paper towels. Fold each round and staple into a round or square custard cup, or use rounds to line oiled rice bowls or ramekins.

Partially fill a wok or pot with water (steamer should not touch water) and bring to a rapid simmer. Mix fish, curry paste, peanuts, coconut cream, eggs, fish sauce, salt and pepper. Fill each banana cup with $1/6$ fish mixture, then $1/6$ shredded cabbage, and place in a bamboo steamer or steamer basket. Cover with double layer of greased plastic wrap or parchment (baking) paper, or place a cloth under lid to stop any condensation dripping onto cups. Place steamer over water, cover, and steam until set, 10–15 minutes. (A skewer inserted in custard will come out clean when cooked.) Garnish with a dollop of coconut cream and sliced chili if desired. Serve hot.

Serves 6

Shrimp and chicken custard

4 dried shiitake mushrooms

5 oz (150 g) skinless, boneless chicken breast, diced

1 teaspoon Japanese soy sauce

1 teaspoon sake (rice wine) or dry white wine

For broth

2½ cups (20 fl oz/625 ml) dashi (bonito stock)

2 teaspoons Japanese soy sauce

1 tablespoon sake (rice wine) or dry white wine

pinch salt

8 medium shrimp (prawns), shelled and deveined

½ cup (2 oz/60 g) sliced carrot, halved

4 spinach leaves, blanched and chopped

4 eggs

julienne of lime or lemon zest, for garnish

Dashi (bonito stock):
Combine 2½ cups (20 fl oz/625 ml) water with 1 teaspoon dashi granules, stirring, until granules dissolve.

Soak mushrooms in warm water for 20 minutes. Drain, gently squeezing to remove excess water. (Do not discard water; it will make a good addition to any stock.) Discard stems, and chop each mushroom into 2 or 3 pieces.

Marinate chicken in soy and sake for 10 minutes.

To make broth: Mix dashi, soy sauce, sake and salt in a small bowl, stirring until salt dissolves. Divide mushrooms, chicken, shrimp, carrot and spinach among 4–6 cups or ramekins (8 fl oz/250 ml each). Lightly beat eggs, but do not allow to become frothy. Stir in broth, mixing well. Pour egg mixture into each cup and garnish with lime zest. Cover with double layer of plastic wrap or place a cloth under lid when covering to stop condensation dripping onto custards. Place cups in large bamboo steamer or steamer basket, and cover.

Partially fill a large wok or pot with water (steamer should not touch water) and bring to a rapid simmer. Place steamer over water, cover, and steam until custard has just set, 15–20 minutes. (A skewer inserted into custard will come out clean when custard is cooked. Custard does not set very firmly.)

Makes 4–6

Mussels with garlic and lime butter

2 lb (1 kg) mussels

½ cup (4 oz/125 g) butter, softened

2 cloves garlic, crushed

2 tablespoons chopped fresh parsley

2 tablespoons chopped fresh chives

1 teaspoon grated lime zest

freshly cracked black pepper to taste

Scrub mussels under cold running water with a nylon pad or stiff brush and pull off hair-like "beards", discarding any mussels that are cracked or do not close when tapped. Place in a large bamboo steamer or steamer basket. In a small bowl, mix butter, garlic, parsley, chives, lime zest and pepper.

Partially fill a large wok or pot with water (steamer should not touch water) and bring to a rapid simmer. Place steamer over water, cover, and steam until mussels open, 4–6 minutes. Remove from steamer, spoon butter mixture into each shell, and serve immediately with a tossed green salad and crusty bread.

Serves 4

Tip: Substitute basil pesto (see page 56) for garlic and lime butter. Or remove mussels from shells and place one or two on an endive (chicory/witloof) leaf, and serve topped with lime butter. Substitute shelled and deveined shrimp (prawns) for mussels.

Spicy tomato and leek shrimp with Hokkien noodles

2 lb (1 kg) uncooked jumbo shrimp
(prawns), shelled and deveined

1 tablespoon olive oil

2 cloves garlic, crushed

1 leek, white part only, sliced and washed

1 small green bell pepper (capsicum),
seeded and diced

2 tablespoons tomato paste

3 large tomatoes (1 lb/500 g), skinned
and chopped

2 teaspoons balsamic vinegar

1 tablespoon chopped fresh basil

1 tablespoon chopped fresh oregano

½ cup (4 fl oz/125 ml) dry white wine

1 lb (500 g) Hokkien noodles (wheat
noodles, available from Asian stores)

Put shrimp in a large bamboo steamer or steamer basket, and cover. Heat olive oil in large saucepan slightly larger in diameter than steamer, and sauté garlic and leek for 2–3 minutes, without browning. Add pepper and tomato paste and cook until paste starts to darken and becomes aromatic, 2–3 minutes. Add tomatoes, vinegar, basil, oregano and wine. Place steamer over pan and steam until shrimp turn pink, 3–6 minutes depending on size. (Remove shrimp from heat and continue to simmer sauce if thicker sauce is preferred.)

Cover noodles with hot water for 1–2 minutes. Drain and separate with a fork, and place in a large bowl. Stir in sauce and shrimp. Serve with a good red wine.

Serves 4

Ginger fish in nori wrapper

For marinade

¼ cup (2 fl oz/60 ml) shaoxing wine or dry sherry

¼ cup (2 fl oz/60 ml) light soy sauce

1 tablespoon fish sauce

1 teaspoon Asian sesame oil

4 fish fillets (snapper, bream, perch, salmon), about 6 oz (185 g) each, and 5–6 inches (12–15 cm) long

8 scallions (shallots/spring onions)

4 sheets toasted nori (yaki-nori or toasted seaweed)

½ red bell pepper (capsicum), seeded and thinly sliced

3 tablespoons Japanese pickled ginger

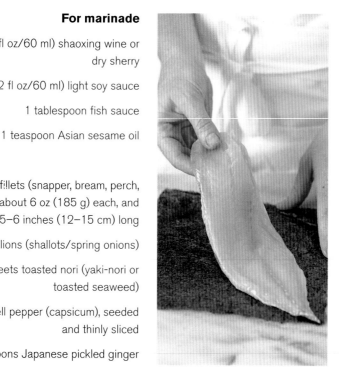

Mix wine, soy sauce, fish sauce and sesame oil in a bowl, and pour over fish fillets in a flat dish. Leave for 20–30 minutes, turning once. Drain, discarding marinade.

Cut scallions into same length as fish fillets, leaving some green top on. Lay each fillet diagonally across a sheet of nori. If nori is too big for fillets, trim to smaller square shape. Place 2 or 3 strips of bell pepper and slices of pickled ginger down center of fish fillet. Add 2 scallions, with one green tip and one white tip at each end. Lightly brush each side flap of nori with water and fold over fish towards center, pressing gently to seal. Fish and vegetable strips will still be visible at either end. Place 2 fish on each level of steamer, and cover.

Partially fill a large wok or pot with water (steamer should not touch water) and bring to a rapid simmer. Place steamer over water and steam until fish flakes when tested with fork and flesh is opaque, 5–8 minutes, depending on thickness of fillets. Switch steamer levels halfway through for even cooking. Remove fish from steamer and serve with remaining pickled ginger and steamed rice.

Serves 4

Calamari salad with lime and chili dressing

1 lb (500 g) cleaned calamari tubes, sliced $\frac{1}{2}$ inch (12 mm) thick

2$\frac{1}{2}$ tablespoons fresh lemon juice

2 cloves garlic, crushed

1 small red chili, seeded and chopped

1 small red chili, finely chopped

2 tablespoons fish sauce

2$\frac{1}{2}$ tablespoons fresh lime juice

1 tablespoon packed light palm or brown sugar

$\frac{1}{2}$ teaspoon Asian sesame oil

2 scallions (shallots/spring onions), finely chopped

1 English (hothouse) cucumber, seeded and chopped

$\frac{1}{4}$ cup ($\frac{1}{3}$ oz/10 g) chopped fresh cilantro (fresh coriander)

$\frac{1}{4}$ cup ($\frac{1}{3}$ oz/10 g) chopped fresh mint

3 cups (3 oz/90 g) mixed green salad

1–2 tablespoons fried garlic chips

Variations: Instead of slicing, cut calamari tubes open along one side, make shallow cuts in a criss-cross pattern on outside, and then cut into $\frac{3}{4}$-inch (2-cm) strips. When cooked, the flesh will curl.

Place calamari in a bowl with lemon juice, garlic and seeded and chopped chili, and marinate for 30 minutes. Drain. Place calamari in a bamboo steamer or steamer basket.

Partially fill a wok or pot with water (steamer should not touch water) and bring to a rapid simmer. Place steamer over water, cover, and steam until calamari is opaque, 3–4 minutes. Remove from steamer and let cool.

Combine finely chopped chili, fish sauce, lime juice, palm sugar and sesame oil in a small bowl, stirring until sugar dissolves. Combine calamari, scallions, cucumber, cilantro and mint, and add chili mixture. Toss to mix well. Arrange on salad leaves, garnished with fried garlic chips.

To make garlic chips: In a small saucepan over medium heat, heat 1 cup (8 fl oz/250 ml) vegetable oil, and fry 10–15 thinly sliced cloves garlic until golden brown and crisp, 2–3 minutes. Be careful not to burn. Can be made ahead and stored in an airtight container. Use garlic oil for frying or seasoning other dishes.

Serves 4

Sizzling teriyaki and ginger fish in banana leaves

4 whole snappers, 8–12 oz (250–375 g) each

2 tablespoons Asian sesame oil

2 stalks lemongrass, white part only, trimmed

1 bunch fresh cilantro (fresh coriander), stemmed

¼ cup peeled and finely julienned fresh ginger

8 scallions (shallots/spring onions), cut into ¾-inch (2-cm) diagonal slices

1 small red bell pepper (capsicum), seeded and thinly sliced

2 banana leaves, softened and halved

¾ cup (6 fl oz/180 ml) peanut oil

¼ cup (2 fl oz/60 ml) Japanese teriyaki sauce

chopped fresh cilantro (fresh coriander) for garnish

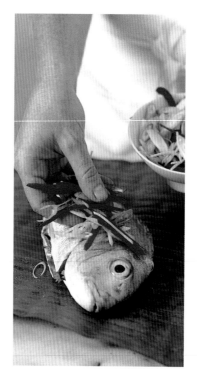

Rub fish inside and out with sesame oil. Make 2 or 3 diagonal cuts through thickest part of flesh on each side of fish. Cut lemongrass to fit inside fish and bruise lemongrass by hitting with knife or meat mallet. Place one half inside fish, along with ¾ cilantro. Scatter ginger, scallions and pepper over each fish, and wrap in softened banana leaf. Place 2 fish in each level of a 12-inch (30-cm) bamboo steamer or steamer basket and cover.

To soften banana leaves: Remove hard stems and drop banana leaves into hot water for 30–60 seconds. Drain and pat dry with paper towels.

Partially fill wok or pot with water (steamer should not touch water) and bring to a rapid simmer. Place two-level steamer over boiling water and steam 15–20 minutes, depending on size, or until fish flakes when tested with a fork and is opaque. Switch level of steamer halfway through for even cooking.

Lift fish parcels out of steamer and place on serving plates. Heat peanut oil in a small saucepan until it smokes, and immediately pour over each fish. This will make a great sizzling sound. Drizzle teriyaki sauce over fish and garnish with chopped cilantro.

Serves 4

Vegetables and salads

Steaming is one of the best methods for cooking vegetables. The method is the same for most vegetables; only the time varies. Put washed vegetables in a bamboo steamer or steamer basket. Partially fill a wok or pot with water (steamer should not touch the water) and bring to a rapid simmer. Place the steamer over the water, cover, and steam until vegetables are cooked. Line bamboo steamers with cheesecloth (muslin) or parchment (baking) paper if small vegetables could fall through the bamboo slats.

Make a selection of vegetables with similar cooking times, cut them into similar-sized pieces, and steam until just tender. Toss with butter, olive oil, lemon juice, balsamic vinegar or soy sauce. Garnish with toasted sesame seeds, chopped fresh herbs, toasted bread crumbs, sliced scallions or toasted nuts.

Here is a guide to steaming vegetables.

2–4 minutes: Asian greens such as bok choy, Shanghai bok choy, choy sum (2–3 minutes or until leaves are wilted); Chinese broccoli (gai lan; 3–4 minutes or until stems are tender); Chinese cabbage and spinach; mushrooms; snow peas; sliced zucchini

4–8 minutes: Asparagus; fava (broad) beans, sugar snap peas, peas; broccoli and cauliflower florets; carrots and parsnips, sliced; potatoes and sweet potatoes, diced or sliced; cabbage and swiss chard (silverbeet); corn on the cob; brussels sprouts

8–15 minutes: Potatoes and sweet potatoes, overlapped slices, 10–15 minutes; baby new potatoes, 12–18 minutes; celery root (celeriac), diced

15 minutes or more: Eggplant (aubergine), whole or half; potatoes, whole; beets (beetroots), whole (15–20 minutes if small, 35–45 minutes if large)

Garlic mashed potatoes

4 unpeeled cloves garlic

3–4 (1 1/4 lb/625 g) russet (baking) potatoes, peeled and cut into 1/2-inch (12-mm) pieces

1/2–3/4 cup (4–6 fl oz/125–180 ml) milk, heated

2 tablespoons butter, softened

1–2 tablespoons chopped fresh chives

salt and freshly ground black pepper to taste

1 tablespoon heavy (double) cream, optional

Place garlic in a frying pan over medium-low heat. Cook until cloves are soft and skins are lightly browned, 10–12 minutes, moving pan occasionally to prevent garlic burning. Leave until cool to touch. Squeeze garlic out of skins and mash with a fork.

Place potatoes in bottom level of a bamboo steamer or a steamer basket lined with cheesecloth (muslin), and cover. Partially fill a wok or pot with water (steamer should not touch water) and bring to a rapid simmer. Put steamer over water, cover, and steam until potatoes are tender, 6–8 minutes. Heat milk in a small saucepan or a microwave or, if using a two-level bamboo steamer, put milk in a heatproof bowl, cover with plastic wrap, and place on level above potatoes to heat through.

Remove potatoes from steamer, put in a bowl, and mash with a whisk or fork. Gradually stir in butter, chives, garlic, salt and pepper, then enough hot milk and cream, if desired, for a creamy consistency. Keep warm by covering with plastic wrap and placing in a covered steamer over simmering water until needed.

Serves 4

Corn on the cob

4 fresh ears corn, husks removed

Marinade no. 1:

1 tablespoon light soy sauce

1 tablespoon olive oil

1/2 teaspoon Asian sesame oil

1 clove garlic, crushed

Marinade no. 2:

1 tablespoon sweet chili sauce

1 teaspoon fish sauce

1/2 teaspoon Asian sesame oil

1 clove garlic, crushed

1 teaspoon grated lemon or
Szechwan pepper

2 tablespoons chopped fresh cilantro
(fresh coriander)

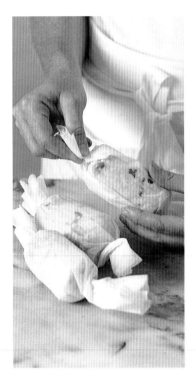

Try one of these marinades to give corn on the cob a different flavor.

Combine marinade ingredients in a shallow dish and pour over corn. Refrigerate for several hours or overnight, turning corn occasionally. Wrap each cob in parchment (baking) paper, twisting the ends to seal. Cook in a covered steamer over rapidly simmering water until tender, 6–8 minutes.

Serves 4

Baby potatoes with lemon dill butter
Green beans with macadamia and garlic butter

For potatoes

1 $\frac{1}{2}$ lb (750 g) unpeeled baby
potatoes, washed

1–2 tablespoons butter

1 teaspoon grated lemon zest

1–2 tablespoons chopped fresh dill
or parsley

freshly ground black pepper to taste

For green beans

12 oz (375 g) green beans, trimmed

freshly ground black pepper to taste

1–2 tablespoons butter

$\frac{1}{2}$ cup (2$\frac{1}{2}$ oz/75 g) toasted macadamia
nuts, coarsely chopped

2 cloves garlic, crushed

Put potatoes in a bamboo steamer or steamer
basket. Partially fill a wok or pot with water
(steamer should not touch water) and bring to a
rapid simmer. Put steamer over water, cover, and
steam until potatoes are tender, 12–18 minutes,
depending on size. (Potatoes are done when easily
pierced with a skewer.) Toss potatoes with butter
and zest, and dill or parsley. Sprinkle with pepper.

Serves 4–6

To make green beans: Put beans in a bamboo
steamer or steamer basket. Partially fill a wok or
pot with water (steamer should not touch water)
and bring to a rapid simmer. Put steamer over
water, cover, and steam until beans are cooked
but still firm, 4–5 minutes. Transfer beans to a
bowl and sprinkle with pepper.

While beans are cooking, melt butter in a small
saucepan, add nuts and garlic, and brown lightly.
Remove from heat and pour over beans.

Serves 4

Stuffed zucchini blossoms

2 scallions (shallots/spring onions),
finely sliced

1 clove garlic, finely chopped

1 cup (5 oz/150 g) cooked rice

3 tablespoons grated Parmesan

2 tablespoons chopped fresh parsley

2 tablespoons chopped fresh dill

1 small tomato (3 oz/90 g), seeded

2 teaspoons capers

salt and freshly ground pepper to taste

2 eggs, separated

12–16 zucchini (courgette) blossoms

balsamic vinegar for sprinkling

Mix scallions, garlic, rice, cheese, parsley, dill, tomato, capers, salt and pepper in a bowl. In another bowl, lightly beat egg yolks, then stir into rice mixture. In a large bowl, beat egg whites until soft peaks form. Gently fold into rice mixture. Hold zucchini blossoms open and fill each one three-fourths full with rice mixture, folding petals over to hold mixture in.

Partially fill a wok or pot with water (steamer should not touch water) and bring to a rapid simmer. Line a 12-inch (30-cm) bamboo steamer or steamer basket with parchment (baking) paper or banana leaves, and carefully place zucchini blossoms in a circle. Place over water, cover, and steam until cooked, 6–8 minutes. (Zucchini is done when easily pierced with a skewer.) Serve hot or at room temperature as an entrée, with a sprinkling of balsamic vinegar.

Makes 12–16 (allow 2–3 per person depending on blossom size)

Zucchini with chicken and shiitake

2 dried shiitake mushrooms

1 giant zucchini (courgette) or Asian fuzzy (hairy) melon (about 1 1/4 lb/625 g), peeled

8 oz (250 g) ground (minced) chicken

2 scallions (shallots/spring onions), finely chopped

2 tablespoons chopped canned bamboo shoots

1 clove garlic, minced

1 tablespoon light soy sauce

1 teaspoon shaoxing wine

1/2 teaspoon Asian sesame oil

1 teaspoon peeled and grated fresh ginger

For sauce

1/2 cup (4 fl oz/125 ml) chicken stock

2 tablespoons oyster sauce

1 medium red chili, seeded and finely chopped, optional

3 teaspoons cornstarch (cornflour)

1 teaspoon water

snow pea (mange-tout) shoots for garnish, optional

Soak mushrooms in hot water for 15 minutes. Drain, gently squeezing out excess water. Discard stems and finely chop tops.

Cut zucchini into 1-inch (2.5-cm) slices and scoop out seeds with a teaspoon. Combine mushrooms, chicken, scallions, bamboo shoots, garlic, soy sauce, wine, sesame oil and ginger in a bowl, mixing well. Spoon approximately 2 tablespoons chicken mixture into the center of each zucchini slice, mounding the mixture 1/2 inch (12 mm) above the slice. Place slices on individual pieces of parchment (baking) paper, and place in a 12-inch (30-cm) bamboo steamer or steamer basket. (If using a two-level steamer, switch levels halfway through for even cooking.)

Partially fill a wok or pot with water (steamer should not touch water) and bring to a rapid simmer. Place steamer over water, cover, and steam until melon is tender, 10–15 minutes.

To make sauce: Heat stock, oyster sauce and chili in a small saucepan. Mix cornstarch and water, then stir in 1 tablespoon hot stock. Add to remaining stock, stirring constantly until thickened.

Serve zucchini slices with sauce poured over, and garnished with snow pea shoots, or on a bed of garlic mashed potatoes (see page 80).

Serves 4 as a starter or light lunch with salad

Asparagus with wasabi mayonnaise

2 bunches fresh asparagus

2–3 cups (2–3 oz/60–90 g) baby arugula (rocket) or baby spinach leaves

For wasabi mayonnaise

2 egg yolks

2½ tablespoons fresh lemon juice

pinch salt and freshly ground black pepper

¾ cup (6 fl oz/180 ml) olive oil

2 teaspoons wasabi paste, or to taste

2 scallions (shallots/spring onions), green part only, thinly sliced

Variations: Omit wasabi and add pesto (see page 56), or add extra garlic for a delicious garlic mayonnaise. Or serve asparagus hot or at room temperature, sprinkled with olive oil and balsamic vinegar, and topped with shaved Parmesan and freshly ground black pepper.

Wash asparagus and trim or snap off woody base. (Young, thin asparagus should snap when bent where woodiness begins. Peel lower part of thick asparagus with a knife or vegetable peeler.) Place in a bamboo steamer or steamer basket.

Partially fill wok or pot with water (steamer should not touch water) and bring to a rapid simmer. Place steamer over water, cover, and steam until asparagus is tender but still crisp, 5–10 minutes depending on thickness. Immediately drop into cold water to stop cooking. Arrange asparagus on arugula leaves.

To make wasabi mayonnaise: Combine egg yolks, lemon juice, salt and pepper in a blender and process until smooth. With machine running, gradually add oil in a thin stream, slowly at first until mixture begins to thicken, then faster. Stir in wasabi, mixing well until no lumps remain.

Serve as an entrée or salad, with wasabi mayonnaise drizzled over and garnished with scallions.

Serves 4–6

Asian greens with tempeh and oyster sauce

1 bunch bok choy or choy sum, trimmed and cut into 4-inch (10-cm) lengths

3 oz (90 g) tempeh or tofu (bean curd), cut into ½-inch (12-mm) pieces

3 oz (90 g) enoki mushrooms, trimmed

3½ oz (100 g) bottled baby corn, halved

¼ cup (2 fl oz/60 ml) oyster sauce

1 clove garlic, crushed

1 teaspoon Asian sesame oil

½ teaspoon peeled and grated fresh ginger

2 scallions (shallots/spring onions), finely chopped

1 tablespoon sesame seeds, toasted (see page 32)

Put bok choy, tempeh, enoki and baby corn in a large bamboo steamer or steamer basket. Partially fill a wok or pot with water (steamer should not touch water) and bring to a rapid simmer. Put steamer over water, cover, and steam until vegetables are softened, 3–4 minutes.

Meanwhile, put oyster sauce, garlic, sesame oil, and ginger in a small saucepan and mix well. Place saucepan over medium heat to warm sauce, 3–4 minutes.

Remove vegetables from steamer and arrange on serving plates with enoki in the center. Drizzle warm sauce over vegetables. Sprinkle with scallions and sesame seeds. Serve as a side dish or light vegetarian dish.

Serves 2–4

Variation: Steam deveined peeled fresh shrimp (prawns) (3–5 minutes) or scallops (2–3 minutes), and toss through bok choy just before serving. Drop 8 oz (250 g) fresh udon or egg noodles into water to cook (2–3 minutes) while vegetables are steaming. Serve noodles with vegetables spooned on top.

Baby beet, orange and toasted almond salad

2 bunches small or medium beets
(beetroots), washed and trimmed

2 oranges, peeled and segmented

1 red (Spanish) onion, thinly sliced

3 cups (3 oz/90 g) mixed salad greens

1/4 cup (1 1/2 oz/50 g) almonds, toasted
and coarsely chopped, for garnish

Mint and orange salad dressing

1/2 cup (4 fl oz/125 ml) freshly squeezed
orange juice

1/4 cup (2 fl oz/60 ml) olive oil

1/4 cup (2 fl oz/60 ml) rice vinegar

1 tablespoon chopped fresh mint

salt and freshly ground pepper to taste

Put beets in a bamboo steamer or steamer basket.
Partially fill a wok or pot with water (steamer should
not touch water) and bring to a rapid simmer. Place
steamer over water, cover, and steam until beets are
tender, 15–20 minutes (35–45 minutes for medium
size). Test by inserting a skewer into thickest part.
Immerse in cold water until cool enough to handle,
then drain. Gently peel off skin, and halve or slice
beets depending on size. While still warm, toss
with salad dressing, then refrigerate for 1 hour.
Drain beets, reserving dressing.

Arrange beets, orange segments and onion slices
on salad greens. Pour salad dressing over, and
garnish with toasted nuts.

To make salad dressing: In a bowl, mix all
ingredients until well combined.

To toast almonds: Place almonds in a frying pan
over medium heat, and cook until lightly browned,
3–4 minutes. Be careful not to burn.

Serves 4–6

Desserts

It is surprising how many desserts can be prepared by steaming—steamed puddings to cakes, velvety custards and créme brûlée, mousses, rice pudding and even poached fruit or fresh fruit kabobs. For optimum flavor, serve with fresh flavored cream or yogurt, ice cream, custard or wine sauces.

Preparation is very simple: cook in a covered steamer over rapidly simmering water, or directly in the pot, with rapidly simmering water halfway up the sides of the dishes. Many such desserts can be prepared ahead and refrigerated until required.

A two-level steamer can be used to prepare a sauce at the same time as the dessert, or the dessert at the same time as the main course. If the dessert is covered (with aluminum foil for example), the flavors of the dessert and main course will not mix. Simple and delicious!

Remember to pleat the parchment (baking) paper before covering puddings to allow for expansion, and to place a kitchen towel under the lid to absorb any condensation before it drips onto the food. Pleating parchment (baking) paper is simply putting a pleat in the paper before placing it over the food that is to be steamed. This allows food to expand and prevents it from being squashed by the paper when it expands.

When using ramekins, tie a piece of string with a loop around the rim of ramekins, especially if using a deep pot, for easy removal of hot dishes without burning yourself. The ramekins called for in this section, are 8 oz (250 ml) in capacity and they can be substituted with medium-sized Chinese teacups. Using Chinese teacups is great for serving at large parties and gatherings.

Grand Marnier crème caramels

⅓ cup (2½ oz/80 g) granulated sugar

3 tablespoons water

4 eggs

2 tablespoons superfine (caster) sugar

2½ cups (20 fl oz/625 ml) milk

1 teaspoon vanilla extract

1 tablespoon Grand Marnier

1 teaspoon grated orange zest

Combine granulated sugar and 3 tablespoons water in a small saucepan and melt sugar over low heat, stirring constantly. Increase heat and boil until mixture caramelizes to a golden brown color, 4–5 minutes. Be careful not to let it burn. Immediately pour into 6 small ramekins 8 oz (250 ml) in diameter, while tipping each dish to cover sides with caramel.

Beat eggs and superfine sugar together until well combined. Stir in milk, vanilla, Grand Marnier and zest. Pour custard into ramekins and cover with oiled aluminum foil or a double layer of plastic wrap.

Partially fill a 12-inch (30-cm) wok or pot with water (steamer should not touch water) and bring to a rapid simmer. Put ramekins in 2 stacked bamboo steamers or two-tiered steamer basket. Place steamer over water, cover, and steam until custard has set, about 20 minutes (an inserted skewer will come out clean when custard is cooked). Switch baskets halfway through for even cooking. Remove from steamer and cool to room temperature. Cover each dish with a fresh sheet of plastic wrap, and refrigerate until required

To serve, place a plate over each custard and invert. Serve with fresh berries.

Serves 6

Variation: Substitute lemon or lime rind for orange rind.

Hot mocha and brandied raisin soufflé

For brandy-soaked raisins

⅓ cup (2 oz/60 g) raisins

1 cup (8 fl oz/250 ml) brandy

4 oz (125 g) dark chocolate

¼ cup (2 oz/60 g) superfine (caster) sugar

4 eggs, separated and 1 extra egg white

1 teaspoon instant coffee granules

⅓ cup (3 fl oz/90 ml) brandy-soaked raisins

Variation: Use Chinese teacups instead of ramekins to make smaller individual soufflés. If they do not all fit in steamer either use two stacked steamers, rotating halfway through for even cooking or whisk half egg whites and cook half the mixture at a time.

Place raisins in an airtight jar and cover with brandy. Cover jar and soak overnight. Drain to use.

Lightly butter six 8-oz (250-ml) ramekins or a 6-cup (48-fl oz/1.5 L) soufflé dish. Put chocolate in a bowl and place bowl in a bamboo steamer or steamer basket. Place uncovered, over wok or pot of simmering water, to melt chocolate. Remove from heat and add sugar, stirring until dissolved. Lightly beat 4 egg yolks and coffee and stir into chocolate, mixing gently. In a large bowl, beat 5 egg whites until stiff, glossy peaks form. Stir one-third of egg whites into chocolate mixture, then lightly fold in remaining whites. Drain raisins and divide them among prepared ramekins. Spoon chocolate mixture onto raisins. Cover each ramekin with a piece of buttered parchment (baking) paper or buttered plastic wrap.

Partially fill a 12-inch (30-cm) wok or pot with water (steamer should not touch water) and bring to a rapid simmer. Arrange ramekins on both levels of a two-level steamer, or large soufflé dish on one level. Place over water, cover, and steam until set, 12–15 minutes (switch levels halfway through for even cooking), although soufflé will still be slightly sticky inside. Serve immediately, or refrigerate and serve chilled.

Makes 6 small soufflés or 1 large

Mini Christmas puddings

2 lb (1 kg) dried mixed fruit

1 cup (8 fl oz/250 ml) brandy, whiskey or rum

1/3 cup (2 oz/60 g) candied cherries

1/3 cup (2 oz/60 g) candied ginger, chopped

1 cup (7 oz/220 g) dark brown sugar, firmly packed

1 tablespoon molasses or dark treacle

grated zest of 1 orange

grated zest of 1 lemon

4 eggs, lightly beaten

1 cup (8 oz/250 g) butter, melted and cooled

1 1/2 cups (7 1/2 oz/235 g) all-purpose (plain) flour, sifted

1/2 cup (2 1/2 oz/75 g) self-rising flour, sifted

2 tablespoons mixed spice powder

6 ramekins, 8 oz (250 ml) capacity each, or 4 cup pudding bowls

Grease each ramekin. Cut two rounds of parchment (baking) paper to fit inside base. Combine dried fruit and liquor in a bowl and cover tightly with a double layer of plastic wrap. Let soak overnight, stirring once or twice.

Place soaked fruit in a large bowl and add cherries, ginger, sugar, molasses, orange and lemon zest and eggs. Mix well and stir in butter, flour and spices. Spoon mixture into each ramekin, up to 1 inch (2.5 cm) above rim. Smooth with the back of a spoon. Cut 6 sheets of parchment (baking) paper and foil, each 12 inches (30 cm) square. Lay paper over foil and fold a pleat in center. Place one piece of paper and foil on top of each pudding, pushing foil over ramekin to seal, and tie with string. Make a loop of string for easy removal of hot puddings from saucepan. Add enough hot water to come halfway up sides of ramekins and steam until cooked, about 1 hour. Add extra simmering water to saucepan if needed.

When puddings are completely cold, remove from ramekins, discarding foil and paper. Place in an oven bag and tie tightly with string, then cover string with a decorative Christmas ribbon and bow.

Makes 6 ramekins or 4 cup pudding bowls

Chinese lemon, date and walnut cake

4 eggs

⅔ cup (5 oz/150 g) sugar

2 teaspoons grated lemon zest

1 cup (5 oz/150 g) all-purpose (plain) flour, sifted

2 tablespoons coarsely chopped walnuts

2 tablespoons coarsely chopped dates

½ teaspoon ground cinnamon

Put eggs in a bowl and beat until frothy, about 2 minutes. Add half of sugar and beat until light and fluffy, 2–3 minutes. Add remaining sugar and lemon zest and beat for 10 minutes.

Gradually stir flour into egg mixture. Do not add too quickly, or flour will sink to bottom. Grease a 9-inch (23-cm) square pan, and spoon in half the mixture. Sprinkle with half of nuts and dates and carefully spoon in remaining egg mixture. Sprinkle top with remaining nuts and dates, then cinnamon. Cover pan loosely, to allow for rising, with a double layer of greased plastic wrap or parchment (baking) paper, or place a kitchen towel under steamer lid to keep any condensation from falling on cake. Place in a large steamer and cover.

Partially fill a wok or pot with water (steamer should not touch water) and bring to a rapid simmer. Place over water, cover, and steam until a skewer inserted in cake comes out clean, about 15 minutes. Cut large cake into squares or slices and serve warm or cold with fresh fruit or fruit coulis and fresh cream.

Makes 1 9-inch square cake

Glossary

Bamboo leaves: Long, narrow leaves available dried from Asian food stores. Leaves impart subtle flavor to food, but are not eaten. Soak briefly in boiling water to soften before use.

Bamboo shoots: Tender but crisp shoots, available in cans from most stores. Used for texture rather than flavor.

Banana leaves: Large, flexible, green, but inedible leaves, used throughout Asia as disposable plates and for wrapping food to be baked or steamed. Available fresh from Asian food stores. Best to use within 7 days.

Bok choy: Asian green vegetable, also known as Chinese cabbage, with thick white stems and mild-flavored dark green leaves. Baby bok choy and Shang hai bok choy are also available. All can be substituted in recipes by Chinese broccoli, choy sum, or other leafy greens.

Chinese broccoli: also known as *gai laan*, with slightly bitter flavor. Discard old or yellow leaves.

Shaoxing wine: Chinese rice wine that is aged for at least 10 years. Can be substituted with dry sherry. Available from Asian food stores.

Chinese dried mushrooms: These are strongly-flavored so use sparingly. Soak in hot water for 15–20 minutes to reconstitute. Discard hard stems and squeeze excess water before use.

Choy sum: Asian green vegetable with yellow flowers and thin stems, also known as flowering cabbage. Whole plant can be lightly steamed and eaten.

Cilantro: Also known as coriander or Chinese parsley. Available fresh, the roots, stems and leaves are all used in cooking, but as they are strongly flavored, use sparingly.

Fish sauce: Pungent, strong-flavored, salty sauce, extracted from salted fish. It's used to enhance and add depth of flavor to dishes. Like wine, flavor and saltiness differ with different brands.

Five-spice powder: A mixture of five spices of equal parts—cinnamon, cloves, fennel seed, star anise and szechuan pepper.

Gow gee press: A plastic utensil for making gow gee or dumplings. Available from Asian food stores.

Hoisin sauce: Sweet, thick, Chinese barbecue sauce, made from soybeans, vinegar, sugar, chili and seasonings. Keeps well if refrigerated once opened.

Hokkien noodles: Fat, round, thick wheat noodles, usually dark yellow and available fresh from Asian stores.

Japanese pickled ginger (*gari*): Thinly sliced, young ginger that has been pickled in sweet vinegar. Used with sushi and sashimi. Pickled older ginger, (*beni shoga*), usually less sweet, is also available from Asian food stores.

Kaffir lime leaves: Unusual double green leaf on one stem with very intense citrus flavor. Although available fresh, frozen or dried, nothing equals the unique and stronger flavor of the fresh. Use whole to infuse flavor, discarding before serving, or remove hard stems and finely cut with scissors before use. Keep refrigerated.

Kaffir lime zest: These look like limes with measles. Finely grate just the green skin for a strong citrus flavor. Although available fresh or frozen from Asian food stores, only use frozen when fresh is unavailable as the flavor is not as intense.

Lemongrass: Long, woody stems with a strong lemon flavor. Discard top green section and root, peel loose outer layers of stem and finely chop before use, or bruise stem with knife and cut into short lengths to release flavor, removing before serving. Available fresh from Asian food stores. Wrap and refrigerate for 3 weeks, or freeze.

Nori: Paper-thin sheets of dried seaweed, generally used for wrapping sushi and rice balls or thinly sliced as a garnish. Lightly toast before use or buy already toasted, sold as *yaki-nori*, for a crisp texture. Must be kept airtight.

Udon noodles: Thick wheat noodles, available fresh (ready to use) or dried from Asian food stores.

Palm sugar: Dense, heavy sugar from different varieties of palm. Available from Asian food stores in different shapes, sizes and colors with a rich caramel flavor. Shave sugar off with a sharp knife. Avoid jars as the sugar dries out and is difficult to remove.

Rice paper wrappers: Dried, round wrappers made from rice, available in large and small sizes and used to wrap savory and sweet fillings. Soak or brush with warm water to soften only when ready to use.

Rice vinegar: One of the mildest vinegars, available from Asian stores. Cider vinegar can be substituted but dilute with water as it's too strong.

Seasoned kampyo (also kanpyo) strips: Dried gourd strips that have been softened and cooked in sweet soy. Available in refrigerated packets or cans from Asian food stores. Keep in the refrigerator and use within 2 to 3 days of opening, or freeze.

Seasoned tofu pouches: Sweet soy-flavored tofu (soybean) pouches. They are traditionally stuffed with sushi rice. Seasoned pouches are available in cans or from refrigerated section of Asian food stores. Use within 2 or 3 days after opening or freeze.

Sesame oil, Asian: Strong, aromatic oil from toasted sesame seeds. Used to add nutty flavor to a dish at the end of cooking. Use sparingly as it is strong. Store in a cool, dark cupboard.

Shiitake mushrooms: Available dried or fresh, the dried have a very intense flavor and must be used sparingly. Soak dried in hot water for 15–20 minutes to reconstitute, discard hard stems and squeeze out excess water.

Shrimp paste: Although it has a pungent odor, shrimp paste adds great depth of flavors to a dish. It must be cooked before use to release flavors, so wrap required amount in foil and broil (grill) or oven roast until aromatic, about 5 minutes. Available in jars, cakes and blocks. Wrap securely in plastic wrap and store in an airtight container.

Tamarind (pulp): Soft, dried pulp of the tamarind pod, that tastes like sour prunes. Although available in powder and liquid concentrate, pulp has better flavor. Soak required amount in boiling water for 10 minutes, breaking up with your fingers, drain and discard pulp. Use in curries, marinades and soups. Available from Asian food stores. Keep airtight and refrigerated once open.

Tempeh: Fermented soybean curd with nutty flavor. Can be marinated before use for added flavor. Good meat substitute for vegetarian dishes. Available from Asian food stores.

Thick coconut cream: Thick, rich liquid squeezed from shredded coconut soaked in water. Available in cans or packets from most stores. Keep refrigerated once open and use within 3–4 days, or freeze.

Thin coconut cream: Also known as coconut milk, this is extracted from shredded coconut soaked in water for a second time after coconut cream is removed. Keep as for coconut cream. Lite coconut milk, with lower fat content, also available in Asian food stores.

Turmeric: Related to ginger, with a slightly bitter, pungent flavor and intense yellow-orange color. Used to add flavor and color to dishes. Available fresh and dried from stores. Refrigerate fresh.

Wasabi: Very hot, lime-green Japanese horseradish. Available as paste in a tube, which should be refrigerated once opened, or powder that is mixed with cold water to desired consistency, but only as required.

Wonton and pot sticker (gow gee) wrappers: Small pliable square or round sheets of dough made from flour, egg and salt, available in various thickness. Used to wrap savory and sweet fillings. Available refrigerated or frozen. Use refrigerated packs within 7 days.

Guide to weights and measures

The conversions given in the recipes in this book are approximate. Whichever system you use, remember to follow it consistently, thereby ensuring that the proportions are consistent throughout a recipe.

Weights

Imperial	Metric
1/3 oz	10 g
1/2 oz	15 g
3/4 oz	20 g
1 oz	30 g
2 oz	60 g
3 oz	90 g
4 oz (1/4 lb)	125 g
5 oz (1/3 lb)	150 g
6 oz	180 g
7 oz	220 g
8 oz (1/2 lb)	250 g
9 oz	280 g
10 oz	300 g
11 oz	330 g
12 oz (3/4 lb)	375 g
16 oz (1 lb)	500 g
2 lb	1 kg
3 lb	1.5 kg
4 lb	2 kg

Volume

Imperial	Metric	Cup
1 fl oz	30 ml	
2 fl oz	60 ml	1/4
3	90 ml	1/3
4	125 ml	1/2
5	150 ml	2/3
6	180 ml	3/4
8	250 ml	1
10	300 ml	1 1/4
12	375 ml	1 1/2
13	400 ml	1 2/3
14	440 ml	1 3/4
16	500 ml	2
24	750 ml	3
32	1L	4

Useful conversions

1/4 teaspoon	1.25 ml
1/2 teaspoon	2.5 ml
1 teaspoon	5 ml
1 Australian tablespoon	20 ml (4 teaspoons)
1 UK/US tablespoon	15 ml (3 teaspoons)

Butter/Shortening

1 tablespoon	1/2 oz	15 g
1 1/2 tablespoons	3/4 oz	20 g
2 tablespoons	1 oz	30 g
3 tablespoons	1 1/2 oz	45 g

Oven temperature guide

The Celsius (°C) and Fahrenheit (°F) temperatures in this chart apply to most electric ovens. Decrease by 25°F or 10°C for a gas oven or refer to the manufacturer's temperature guide. For temperatures below 325°F (160°C), do not decrease the given temperature.

Oven description	°C	°F	Gas Mark
Cool	110	225	1/4
	130	250	1/2
Very slow	140	275	1
	150	300	2
Slow	170	325	3
Moderate	180	350	4
	190	375	5
Moderately Hot	200	400	6
Fairly Hot	220	425	7
Hot	230	450	8
Very Hot	240	475	9
Extremely Hot	250	500	10

Index

First published in the United States in 2000 by Periplus Editions (HK) Ltd.,
with editorial offices at 153 Milk Street, Boston, Massachusetts 02109 and
5 Little Road #08-01 Singapore 536983

Library of Congress Cataloguing-in-Publication Data is available.
ISBN 962-593-940-7

DISTRIBUTED BY

USA
Tuttle Publishing
Distribution Center
Airport Industrial Park
364 Innovation Drive
North Clarendon, VT 05759-9436
Tel: (802) 773-8930
Tel: (800) 526-2778

Japan
Tuttle Publishing
RK Building, 2nd Floor
2-13-10 Shimo-Meguro, Meguro-Ku
Tokyo 153 0064
Tel: (03) 5437-0171
Fax: (03) 5437-0755

Asia Pacific
Berkeley Books Pte. Ltd.
5 Little Road #08-01
Singapore 53698
Tel: (65) 280-3320
Fax: (65) 280-6290

Set in Akzidenz Grotesk on QuarkXPress
Printed in Singapore by Tien Wah Press

First Edition
06 05 04 03 02 01 00 10 9 8 7 6 5 4 3 2 1